FRICTION IN U.S. FOREIGN POLICY:
CULTURAL DIFFICULTIES WITH THE WORLD

> Among key transformational insights is the necessity to deal with the world as it is—not as it used to be and not as we wish it were. Sound strategic thinking recognizes the limits of our intelligence, in all senses of the term.
>
> Douglas J. Feith,
> Under Secretary of Defense for Policy

America's ability to remain in a world leadership role has never before depended so much on being able to influence foreign populations. Yet in the years since the end of the Cold War, the world has witnessed a sharp rise in anti-Americanism: "Anti-Americanism is now like a religion around the world."[2] Such hostility and resentment comes largely as a result of trying to transplant, too directly, culture that works in America to the rest of the world. It is intuitive for most Americans to feel that modernity and the pursuit of individual liberties are the only viable way for humanity to progress. Yet Americans might well be blind to what the rest of the world thinks and ignorant of competitive culturally diverse alternatives. Such lack of comprehension in a world where the U.S. population is a distinct minority risks America's future. The United States must determine how to bring about the future it envisions in a world that is increasingly hostile. America today is confronted with several competing non-Western ideologies that Americans seem culturally blind to acknowledging. These competing ideologies are rooted in growing world cultural differences with the West, as alluded to in *Arab News.com* by a female Saudi reporter based in Jeddah, Saudi Arabia:

> For too long the world has lived with one dominant culture imposing its view on everyone else. . . . The West can't for the moment come to grips with the fact that they occupy this planet with other individuals who have a different set of values which are as true as theirs. Muslims are not the only ones who feel the intrusive and high-handed behaviour of the West. We see examples of this kind of attitude all around the world from Latin America to Africa and Asia.[3]

Success in promoting the U.S. worldview, and winning the Global War on Terror (GWOT) specifically, rests in Americans recognizing their own cultural uniqueness and developing a high level of cultural savvy in dealing with more traditional cultures. The United States can find more attainable foreign policy success using indirect strategies, though this would be against prevailing instincts.[4] With cultural savvy, the United States can apply the spirit of Colonel T. E. Lawrence: "Better to let them do it imperfectly than to do it perfectly yourself, for it is their country, their way, and our time is short."[5]

A key part of a constructive grand strategy is in seeing the "world as it is—not as it used to be and not as we wish it were."[6] "Seeing the world as it is" is a part of the competency of strategic objectivity— seeing the reality and what is realistic and attainable over time." Cultural savvy allows the United States to see with strategic objectivity and act in a manner reflecting cultural astuteness.

THE WORLD THE UNITED STATES ENVISIONS

Americans tend to believe that since the United States led the free world to victory over the Soviet Union in the Cold War, it will continue as the leader of a free and democratic world modeled after itself. One can see this optimism in the George W. Bush administration's 2002 National Security Strategy (NSS):

> The great struggles of the 20th century between liberty and totalitarianism ended with a decisive victory for the forces of freedom—and a single sustainable model for national success: Freedom, democracy, and free enterprise.[7]

Such presumption tends to explain every opposition in dramatic terms of "good and evil" and see others as either with us or against us. Often, such language is directed at a world audience but is cloaked in U.S. historical and cultural experience.[8] Labeling "black and white" in the modernizing world can be extremely challenging when most transnational issues are more in the "grey" area and involve traditional cultures. For example, sorting out good and evil regarding radical Islam has proved a vexing problem for western leaders who attempt to delink extremists from nonextremists, as highlighted by President Bush in describing radical Islam: "The Islamic Radical Threat to this century greatly resembles the bankrupt ideology of the last. The murderous ideology of the Islamic radicals is the greatest challenge of our century. Yet, in many ways, this fight resembles the struggle against Communism in the last century."[9] Only the word "radical" distinguishes the terrorists from 1.2 billion Muslims, many of whom may be nonviolent radicals. "Even support by 1 percent of the Muslim population would equate to over 12 million enemies."[10] President Bush may have overdramatized the radical challenge, but, nonetheless, radical or populist Islam is a grave ideological threat because it appeals to the traditional Islamic cultures of many societies. The United States must learn how to deal with disturbing religious trends, as well as how to promote democracy, without ceding ground to a competing ideology that is inextricably intertwined with a religion. Contemplating such thought is hard for secular bound Americans who traditionally are very averse in discussing "church and state" issues in the context of public diplomacy. It is only slightly less difficult when other ideologies are involved because of the U.S. belief in the right to dissent. Hence, the United States must first understand what its long-term interests are and then how best to pursue them in a world that does not share the U.S. cultural experience.

U.S. interests flow from the Nation's desired worldview for the future. The U.S. worldview can be summarized rather succinctly: To seek a global world order in which the United States can prosper with its values intact. It does not seek direct rule, but the realization of U.S. values suggests a desired world in which the United States is first among equals in a multilateral world, though convincing the world it is not unilateral will require great cultural savvy. Such a world order would be a peaceful global community of democratic societies engaged in fruitful commerce, that respects human rights, freedom of religion, rule of secular law, and the individual pursuit of happiness. This worldview is rooted firmly in a nontraditional American culture that is a product of America's unique historical experience. It is entirely reasonable for the United States to seek to shape a world order favorable to itself and founded in its own experience. Yet, it is problematic in dealing with more traditional cultures where America cannot wish success into being. The big question is how can the United States best pursue the world it seeks? The answer lies in understanding our own culture and that of others, and then acting with objectivity. As Sun Tzu would say: "Know your enemy and know yourself, and in a hundred battles you will never be in peril."[11]

CULTURE CLASH AND INTERESTS JUXTAPOSED

Knowing your enemy is not an historical U.S. strength. Americans generally do not appreciate other societies and cultures, much less "know" them well enough to facilitate accurate predictive analysis. A study of American history shows a pattern of not recognizing subtle clues that portend radical shifts in history, much of it hidden in a cultural context. For example, the United States was surprised by the Japanese attack on Pearl Harbor in 1941, not foreseeing the Japanese military response to the U.S. prewar trade embargo against Japan. The United States and its allies did not appreciate fully the consequences of the rise of Nazi dictator Adolf Hitler, perhaps swayed by the appearance of a German democratic process. Even today, we can see traces of Neville Chamberlain's "peace in our time" through appeasement in how we dealt with the rise of Islamic radicals in the 1990s.[12] The United States did not see the rise of Communism as an enemy of democracy during World War II and, subsequently, failed to foresee the Cold War. The United States failed to foresee the Soviet invasion of Afghanistan in 1980, and did not appreciate the significance of the start of the Islamic "jihad" there, expediently focusing on al-Qa'ida's shared goal with the United States at the time — the defeat of the Soviet Union. Further, the United States failed to anticipate the downfalls of both the Shah of Iran and the Soviet Union, not recognizing when their populations would react and how to support it. Consequently, rampant multilateralism and Islamic fundamentalism, from the latter, continue to hinder the achievement of the U.S. worldview. Each of these events had an ideological component rooted in their peoples' culture.

America is beginning to take note of its cultural alienation in the world, as evidenced by the Presidential State of the Union address on January 31, 2006, and the *Quadrennial Defense Review* of February 6, 2006, both of which recognize the significance of culture in U.S. foreign affairs. Yet, while recognizing culture is significant, neither of these make clear that it is the major strategic consideration. Almost all other cultures are much more traditional than the United States, and many see that as a threat. Western Europe and other modernized societies are threatened, to a lesser degree, than the Third World where U.S. culture challenges every aspect of their lives; but all feel threatened by America's "distinct and positive universal culture based on the dignity of the individual."[13]

The United States still does not appreciate fully at least three major alternative ideologies, founded in distinct cultures, that compete with the Western democratic model and U.S. worldview. First, "radical Islamic extremism" is rapidly becoming "populist Islamic extremism." The United States hopes that extremism will be rejected by a majority of the "uma" or Islamic populace without truly appreciating its populist appeal or the grave ideological threat it poses. From defeating al-Qa'ida and the roots of radical extremism, the U.S. objective has evolved into the larger objective of promoting democratic reform in the Middle East.[14] However well-intended this objective, the evidence suggests it was fashioned without cultural astuteness and without regard for how to mesh democracy with Islam. A *USA Today* front page headline on January 25, 2006, suggested the disturbing possibility that U.S. democratic reforms might either be premature or backfiring: "Mid-East Democracy Boots Islamists; U.S. Pushes Elections/Fundamentalists Gain. Trend Evident in the Region."[15] The United States staunchly has advocated democratic elections, incorrectly thinking that all the "Islamic main-street" wanted was an outlet for dissent. Instead, terrorist organizations have won popular support in 4 of 5 recent elections: in Palestine, Hamas; in Egypt, the Islamic Brotherhood; in Iraq, the Shias with connections to Iran; and in Lebanon, Hezbollah. Pushing for elections before a population is ready for democratic reform without appreciating mosque and state separation does not augur well for favorable democratic results or support of America's worldview. Through lack of cultural understanding, the United States might have prompted election returns reflecting Islamic resentment or pride, as opposed to support for a democratic process. Americans must look at the experiences of others to learn. Within the Islamic world, historical precedents within Turkey suggest Americans should consider promoting intermediate steps to grow effective representative governance. Such steps require tremendous local knowledge to foster successful internal reform, balancing factors like religion, ethnicity, and opposition to the formation of a strong central government against the rule of law, judicial process, minority rights, women's rights, and clear secular separation of "mosque and state." Such obliviousness is not limited to the Islamic world.

Second is a "hybrid Chinese Communist Capitalist" ideology. China is both a major U.S. trade partner and target of American desires for democratic reform. Free trade with China was advocated to promote democratic reforms in this Communist nation, an adversary of the United States since the Communist rise to power in 1949. It was inconceivable to most Americans that China could possibly delink prosperity from democracy. Even now, few can conceive the possibility that China might be able to succeed where every other Communist nation failed. The current U.S. strategy risks being beaten at its own game and winding up behind China, with "blind faith promoting the rise of China and India driving the U.S. economy to second place by 2040."[16] Further, the U.S. free trade policy has allowed the Communist government to rearm massively with modern weapons.[17] To understand Chinese culture is to understand an intense distrust of the outside world as a result of over 100 years of perceived foreign exploitation. China wishes to be a global power superior to the United States, or, for that matter, Japan, Russia, and anyone else. Yet, America thinks it can cut a deal with anyone in the belief other rising powers will find pragmatic reasons to support the U.S. worldview. China, wealthier and more economically influential than the United States, would not be in the interest of world freedom and democracy if it remains an authoritarian culture.

Third, even Latin America and the Western Hemisphere are not locked into an American worldview. A phenomenon that could be labeled "radical populism" championed by Venezuelan President Hugo Chavez is sweeping Latin America. Its cornerstone pillars are rooted in antiglobalization and anti-Americanism. The U.S. Government has been taken by surprise. Democracy has ushered in leftist populist governments in nearly every South American country. Most notable has been the rise of President Chavez, who has demonstrated a personal antipathy toward the United States. Cuba's recalcitrant dictator Fidel Castro "suddenly finds he has more friends than at any time in his 4-plus decades in power, in defiance of the long-standing U.S. trade embargo."[18] Castro and Chavez now have been joined by President Evo Morales of Bolivia, the first ever Indian to rise to be president in any Latin American country.[19] This neo-populist ideology has the potential to spread into the rest of Latin America, ushered in by the democratic election process, which is clearly linked to U.S. policies in the region. Latin American populists routinely complain about what a bad neighbor the United States has been.

Recent policy decisions have compounded the historical record, aggravating relations in the region and further fueling radical populism against the United States. The U.S. policy of cutting off aid to nations who ratify the International Criminal Court (ICC) Treaty on the theoretical chance a U.S. service member might be indicted in some future incident is perceived as an arrogant and unfair reaction to support of the rule of law. With the ICC U.S. aid policy,

> [T]he United States is going out of it is way to punish the region's largest democracies. . . . At the moment, 12 of 21 nations in Latin America have been suspended from U.S. military training and aid programs because of the ICC rule, including Brazil, Peru, Costa Rica, Ecuador, Bolivia, Uruguay . . . and Mexico. . . . Chile will soon ratify the treaty. . . .[20]

Latin Americans make a historical association of "free trade" with "economic exploitation" by the United States. Latin American sensitivities were made very clear to President Bush when he encountered a hostile audience in his bid to expand free trade between the United States and Latin America during his November 4-5, 2005, visit to Mar Del Plata, Argentina:

> The theme of the Fourth Summit of the Americas was to be "Creating Jobs to Fight Poverty and Strengthen Democratic Governance." The Declaration and Plan of Action of Mar del Plata, signed by the attending heads of state and government at the conclusion of the event, was expected to deal extensively with the topic of job creation. Nevertheless, most of the deliberations concerned the Free Trade Area of the Americas (FTAA). . . . In the midst of protests from the civilian population and after opposition from the four Mercosur countries (Brazil, Argentina, Uruguay, and Paraguay) and Venezuela, which maintained that the U.S.-led proposal would damage their nations' economies, the Summit talks failed to reach an agreement on a regional trade deal. . . . Venezuelan President Hugo Chavez pronounced the FTAA "buried."[21]

Some would argue that anti-Americanism is a distracting rhetoric to conceal the root causes of Latin American poverty—a culture of outright corruption and exploitation of the people and land by their own business and intellectual elites.[22] Rather than looking inward, Latin American populists target the United States, which easily falls prey to accusations of U.S. meddling and exploitation by its own lack of cultural savvy. If the United States wants to succeed in building favorable relations in Latin America, it must tailor its approach and understand Latin America's unique dynamics. For example, Latin American populists have so maligned free trade with the United States that any reference to it is tantamount to advocating depressed wages for the working classes for the benefit of U.S. consumers and Latin American oligarchs. Cultural astuteness, in this case, would address how to promote free trade in a more indirect manner, behind successful Latin American leaders better able to promote a mutually symbiotic U.S. agenda. Although the United States has nothing militarily to fear from a leftist resurgence in the region for now, ". . . we are witnessing what the Germans and the Soviets could not achieve—the strategic denial of Latin America to the United States. Latin America promises to be a region fraught with violence, corruption, ecological damage, poverty, and "desgobierno" (misgovernment)."[23]

Not only are there at least three competing ideologies from three distinct cultural groups, but they have shown a willingness to work together against the United States. Cooperation between Communist China and radical populists in Latin America is one example. America cannot ignore a possible correlation between the rise of Chinese economic presence in the Western Hemisphere with a rise in anti-Americanism. Unlike relations with the United States, Chinese policy has no human rights preconditions that might be interpreted as internal meddling. Cooperation and mutual distrust of the United States extends beyond China and Latin America.[24] The outright anti-Americanism of Venezuela's Chavez and Bolivia's Morales is joined by a chorus of anti-American voices in parts of Western Europe and large parts of the Middle East and Asia.[25]

Another example of cooperation gaining public attention is the growing relationship between radical Islam and Latin American organized crime. Paraguay's undergoverned "triborder area" adjacent to Argentina and Brazil is linked to Middle Eastern extremists and has a growing potential for being a nexus with Latin American organized crime—all of which highlight the disconcerting possibilities for terrorists to leverage crime infrastructure to gain access into the United States.[26] Though "radical populism" and organized crime are now distinct from each other, rising anti-Americanism could cause Latin American organized crime figures to be more willing to deal with populist politicians, as well as with Islamic extremists.[27] Such criminals already have bases in the United States. "La Mara Salvatrucha 13" (MS13) has 50,000 gang members in the United States, compromising 29 percent of all gangs reported in the Continental United States. It is "a notorious street gang based in El Salvador [which] has spread rapidly into 32 U.S. states and raised enough concern for the Justice Department to create a new high-level task force to battle it."[28] To counter these ideological threats, the United States must understand the host cultures and apply cultural savvy. But first, it must understand itself and how U.S. culture affects its strategic perspective and conflicts with other cultural perspectives.

A NEW WORLD PARADIGM: U.S. CULTURAL PERSPECTIVE

Americans come from a unique New World historical experience that has shaped a particular cultural paradigm founded on progressive ideology and the practical resolution of problems. This New World paradigm causes the United States to overlook foreign culture instinctively, find universal commonalities, and work pragmatic solutions based on perceived "objective" facts to the extent foreign relations will allow—which makes the United States so often appear culturally inept in the post-Cold War environment. "The Cold War brought together the system of balance and empire and made the world a single whole, unified by a single struggle for supremacy and locked in a single balance of terror."[29] Today, other nations can pursue independent interests and strategies, which present new conditions for U.S. leaders, who must now market American leadership and promote the American worldview without the impending doom of totalitarianism to justify their choices. The first step in strategic objectivity is to understand what one's own culture is and how it affects one's perspective.

American culture is a Western Hemisphere "New World Paradigm" that historically has had the challenge of assimilating immigrants from nearly every culture in the world. In such an environment, any foreign culture is seen as a problem to overcome. U.S. success has come from blurring cultural differences and finding common ground among disparate peoples to produce a "new" American identity. U.S. history is one of breaking down foreign cultures, the opposite of cultural savvy, which is to understand and work within other cultures. No matter how much cultural education Americans receive, the legacy of immigrant and multicultural assimilation resists understanding foreign cultures. The Western Hemisphere New World Paradigm is founded on "American exceptionalism," which promotes the successful integration of immigrants by creating a new common identity, best demonstrated by the bond of a common language—monolingualism.

American exceptionalism is an extremely nationalistic style culture that arose from the success of the U.S. national experience. The United States forged a new and vibrant nation by a uniquely American model for success grounded in several concepts such as upward social and economic mobility, new concepts of social justice and individual liberties under the rule of law, separation of church and state, and successful integration of foreign immigration. As the first "universal nation," one that had to accommodate many diverse immigrants, the United States does not include, to the same degree, the elements of hierarchy, community, tradition, and custom so evident in other cultures.[30] "The U.S. fundamental belief in exceptionalism is its righteousness and moral superiority over other nations."[31] Americans must be sensitive to being perceived as chauvinistic towards more traditional cultures. "Chauvinism—Americans think America is the biggest and the best, the newest and the richest, and all others are a bit slow, old-fashioned, rather poor, and somewhat on the small side."[32] Under this logic, it is argued that everything with the "Old World" is flawed, and everything with the "New World" is superior. By understanding American exceptionalism, the United States can better understand its deep-rooted inclinations and keep from applying "one shoe fits all" solutions. In a sense, the "manifest destiny," which led Americans to conquer the North American continent, has been rekindled, and seeks to reshape the world under American principles of social and economic success. Exceptionalism lies at the heart of America's cultural uniqueness, but other historical experience also shapes its culture.

America's history is one of a search for commonality as a result of the rejection of the Old World and its diverse cultures. This search led to the embracement of a secular culture, which, while respecting all religions, placed emphasis in public life on common, shared symbols. With this common focus, ethnicity and traditional culture became secondary to being an American. Americans asked what can we agree on that makes us Americans? Over time, the commonalities defined American culture and built the expectation that others who wished to be American would buy into this cultural identity. It also established a cultural preference for seeking commonalities as opposed to seeking differences. This cultural trait became so manifest by the 1950s that the 1960s saw a rebellion against it that embraced diversity. The depth of the commonalities mindset in our culture can be gauged by our ongoing need for diversity training.

Another aspect of the New World Western Hemisphere experience common to all the European colonies was the promotion of monolingualism, a key element in immigrant assimilation and forging a common identity. Americans have an international reputation for speaking only English. A common joke is, "What do you call someone who speaks three languages? Trilingual. What do you call someone who speaks two languages? Bilingual. What do you call someone who speaks one language? An American."[33] Yet, America's monolingual nature is central to its own success of forging a common national identity. As has often been noted, it is impossible to identify an American by race, color, creed, religion, or ethnic origin. Americans lack any common visible characteristics, other than the common linguistic bond. But with a common linguistic bond, other more abstract bonds are possible. Monolingualism is both an American domestic strength and a foreign relations and commercial weakness.[34] Nations divided along linguistic lines, such as Belgium (French vs. Flemish), Canada (French vs. English), Spain (Spanish vs. Basque, Catalan, Galician, etc.), and Switzerland (four separate and equal cantons divided by language) demonstrate that, even in advanced first world nations, linguistic divisions define identity and lines of conflict which, in some cases, threaten national integrity. So, America's success at stripping away foreign languages from immigrants through its tried and tested formula for assimilation is a domestic success story. On the other hand, American lack of proficiency in other languages impedes cultural astuteness, by not letting Americans hear the exact words others use, which can telegraph very subtle nuances. As in any language, the specific words we choose can offer very telling clues to hidden meanings, the confidence the speaker might have in giving information, or any number of other nuances.

A modern evolution of the American psyche is "political correctness (PC)." America's value of individual freedom, in conflict with commonalities, has led to a unique outlook in regard to certain issues where stereotyping is a contrary cultural imperative. Americans are distracted constantly by exceptions to every rule and have it ingrained in them not to generalize about people. "Don't judge a book by its cover," as the axiom goes. While this is commendable social engineering domestically, it is simplistic to ignore generalities about people overseas. Being PC makes Americans try to overlook any fault with major religions or major groups and leads us to think that all people pretty much want the same things—basic needs and a chance for prosperity. Traditional cultures are, by definition, collective in outlook, not individual. Americans are just not equipped to be PC at home and not-PC abroad.

The "New World Paradigm" is evident whenever Americans interact with another culture. As a result of American exceptionalism, an engaged America seeks to push onto others what worked for America. It seeks to build commonalities, work out compromises, and shape everything around it in the image of the New World. As a result, Americans tend to look at other cultures and project a mirror-image of how they want to think of themselves, failing to see reality. Cultural savvy means to learn the "Good, the Bad, and the Ugly" of both one's own and the target culture, with a clear understanding of the gaps between the two.

CULTURAL SAVVY

American national purpose and the worldview it acts toward continue to build the globalized world emerging today. It promises an even brighter future for humanity, if American leadership can convince the rest of the world to continue following the American model and resist competing ideologies. But American ineptness in reconciling competing foreign ideas with U.S. goals could yet derail progress. Experience shows U.S. policy to be somewhat blind to other views and sending conflicting signals, often making it look like a threat to traditional societies. Essentially, U.S. policymakers, strategists, and other national security professionals lack competency in cultural savvy.

> Cross-cultural savvy implies that an officer can see perspectives outside his or her own boundaries. It does not imply, however, that the officer abandons the Army or American culture in pursuit of a relativistic worldview. Instead, the future strategic leader is grounded in national and Army values, but is also able to anticipate, understand, and empathize with the values, assumptions, and norms of other groups, organizations, and nations.[35]

Most importantly, leaders in national security must be able to translate this cultural savvy into strategies and actions that protect and advance U.S. interests. Simply said, cultural savvy is the recognition that culture is not neutral, and it requires higher and more mature levels of strategic skills.[36] The nuances of cultural savvy at this level can be illustrated.

Koreans avoid compromise, and yet Americans seek it—cultural biases.[37] However, often cultural savvy can overcome cultural biases. For example, it is essential to understand when negotiating with the Koreans that personal bonds developed over time are critical to negotiations and that, culturally, they are averse to compromising, since they are a "win-lose" culture.[38] In such cultures, there can be no compromise, since compromise is viewed as a loss. Americans come from a "win-win" culture, where both sides can claim victory by ceding ground and achieving resolution. Success is founded on building a long-term relationship and fostering "win-win" solutions. Similarly, Iran is a traditional culture that values "face" and has more patience than the United States—or Europe for that matter. Iran might have learned from the North Korean model for nuclear development.[39] Similar challenges are faced in nuclear negotiations: Iran intentionally exploits Western idealistic hopes of a negotiated compromise simply to prevent Western military action diplomatically and buy more time to pursue their national objective—development of a nuclear device.[40] In dealing with such "win-lose" cultures, the prudent American negotiator needs to come in with extremely detailed preparation in order to gain concessions, avoid falling into the cultural fault of wishing a compromise and losing unnecessary ground, and develop mutual personal respect with the foreign negotiator(s). When he does this, he is applying cultural savvy. Preparation and cultural savvy helps the negotiator impose a "win."

Afghanistan.

Operation ENDURING FREEDOM is a text-book success for being "culturally savvy," in so far as "wining hearts and minds" in an Islamic country, to the extent possible by an outside non-Islamic power. In Afghanistan, the United States learned from Soviet failure. Rather than committing large formations of conventional forces, the United States backed the friendly Northern Alliance. Consequently, Afghan forces led the charge against the Taliban, and the United States turned the hunters into the hunted. U.S. advisors showed incredible cultural savvy when working with the Northern Alliance and newer Afghan coalition members to steer them toward the path of modern democracy, accepting local Islamic adaptations. The nascent democratic Afghan government is on its way to building a representative nation and providing for its own security, despite a resilient Taliban/al-Qa'ida residual movement. Afghanistan is not without its threats to U.S. interests when one considers that a free Afghanistan is now the world's leader in opium production and exportation, but U.S. interests were advanced and a relationship now exists to address the narcotics production issue.

If there is any long-term irony in Afghanistan for the United States, it will likely revolve around the United States being perhaps too accommodating in adapting Western style democracy to an Islamic nation. While U.S. soldiers swear an allegiance to the Constitution of the United States, which is a secular document built upon a Judeo-Christian foundation but not subordinate to it, the Afghan Constitution does just the opposite. The U.S. Constitution provides for the separation of church and state and goes to great length to protect individual liberties. The Afghan Constitution clearly subordinates Afghanistan and all its citizens to the Islamic holy book, and its related civil laws.[41] American soldiers unwittingly fought on behalf of an Afghanistan Constitution, subordinate to Sharia law, that denies freedom of religion as understood by Americans and promotes Islamic theocracy:

> In fact, Article 130 says that, in the absence of an explicit statute or constitutional limit, the Supreme Court should decide "in accord with Hanafi jurisprudence," one of the four main Sunni schools of Sharia. (Some forms of Hanafi law give a women's court testimony only half the weight of a man's.) Supreme Court justices are required to have higher education "in law or Islamic jurisprudence" and, like the president and Cabinet members, must take an oath to "support justice and righteousness in accord with the provisions of the sacred religion of Islam."

> The draft provides no guarantees of religious freedom and says only "other religions are free to perform their religious ceremonies within the limits of the provision of law" (2). Already, as in Iran, the draft outlaws any political party "contrary to the principles of the sacred religion of Islam . . ."(35). If the state declares that its laws and decisions are identical with Islam, then any opposition can be punished as violating Islam. In Afghanistan, this is not a theoretical question.[42]

Iraq.

Operation IRAQI FREEDOM, on the other hand, is the text-book "missed opportunity." While the United States and the "coalition of the willing" won the conventional war quickly, the United States was not ready to seize the peace through a combination of two strategic missteps: lack of "Phase IV" post-hostilities planning; and the "firing of the Iraqi Army," civil service, and police forces.[43] As Sun Tzu advised, "Generally, in war the best policy is to take a state intact; to ruin it is inferior to this."[44] World War II savvy would have recognized the need to plan for the postwar (Phase IV) time frame early with the specific intent of including as many former regime elements as possible in the postwar reconstruction. In World War II, the United States used Japanese and German governance and personnel fairly effectively. While there is little doubt that there were "bad" Baathist elements in some positions, it is likely that the United States confused the local cultural intricacies of being "pro-Saddam" and being employed, leading to no government functioning.[45] In the same manner, the United States confused anti-Saddamism for pro-U.S. sentiment. What was underappreciated was the long-term implications of being "freed" by "infidels" on the culturally proud Muslims when U.S. forces had to occupy the nation. Al-Zarqawi is now hailed in the Muslim mainstreet as the top terrorist leader who is putting in place al-Qa'ida's long campaign to establish an Islamic Caliphate throughout the Middle East, with Iraq at its heart.[46] As Dr. Eliot Cohen, an observer of American strategy, often states, Iraq "requires the rarest of American qualities: patience."[47] It requires more of it, because we fail to grasp the role of cultures.

Egypt.

Egypt is a mixed example of cultural savvy at work. The United States worked with Egypt's President Hosni Mubarak to promote positive internal change leading to its first democratic elections in 2005. As Clausewitz said, if you want to impose your will, ultimately the ". . . country must be occupied."[48] In the U.S. worldview, countries must be "occupied" by friendly governments who do not threaten their neighbors, preferably with democratic governments who respect the liberties of their people. However, recent elections have increased representation of a major radical Islamic group, the Islamic Brotherhood. On the one hand, the United States properly leveraged Egyptian leaders to promote democracy. On the other, the Islamic Brotherhood's gaining in the elections demonstrates that democracy cannot be rushed and suggests cultural savvy has a timing component to it. Other social reforms may have to be implemented before elections produce favorable democratic results. Democracy is more than elections, "it is a system of free and independent institutions. A naïve advocacy of democracy without such institutions may open the way to our worst enemies. . . ."[49]

The United Kingdom.

The United States can learn much from others' experience with cultures. The United Kingdom's (UK) experience over the centuries, insofar as managing local relations using only small-scale forces, is very illustrative. It shows that Western armies can develop and apply cultural perspective.

> . . . that organizational culture is the key to the ability to learn from unanticipated conditions, a variable which explains why the British army successfully conducted counterinsurgency in Malaya but why the American army failed to do so in Vietnam, treating the war instead as a conventional conflict. Nagl concludes that the British army, because of its role as a colonial police force and the organizational characteristics created by its history and national culture, was better able to quickly learn and apply the lessons of counterinsurgency during the course of the Malayan Emergency.[50]

Dealing with foreign national culture in a constructive way was echoed more recently by a senior UK officer: "The UK Army was able to control ridiculously large numbers of people, particularly in India, with small numbers of junior personnel by good personal relations."[51] With a personnel rotation system that encouraged "homesteading" throughout the empire, the UK was able to build a pool of highly talented civilian and military personnel with a near native sense of indigenous issues and intrigue. As such, the UK was very adept at playing one local group against another and pursuing successful ". . . alternative forms of control, and a whole variety of inducements to persuade subject peoples to respect their imperial overlords."[52] Using success as the metric, there is a direct power correlation: cultural savvy = fewer contentious issues and less troops needed.

Another point about the UK success is linguistic. While the UK has been protected by the English Channel from the rest of Europe, their officers historically have spoken a second language—French. British officers were bilingual, even when it was their policy to "make the world England" during the French and Indian War time period.[53] The French language not only facilitated dealing with the noble class of the time, but also gave the British officer corps a window to the world, since French was the *"lingua franca"* of diplomacy before World War II. Britain was able to transform itself for its international role by learning cultural savvy and developing a "dynamic and evolving system, always going forward to new destinies. . . ."[54]

Turkey.

U.S. success as it pursues its worldview also depends on a willingness to learn and adapt to the specific situation. Turkey's experience illustrates this. Turkey often is overlooked as a source of insights for democratic reform in the Islamic world. Yet it is an Islamic nation that has struggled with traditional culture and ideology. No other Islamic nation has modernized and reformed itself along Western democratic lines more than Turkey. Turkey today is a full-fledged North Atlantic Treaty Organization (NATO) member and aspires membership in the European Union (EU). While many would argue that Turkey has a way to go to meet fully the western European standards for entrance, it has integrated Islam into a modern democratic nation. To succeed, modern Turkey focused on delinking Islam from the state and politics:

> Kemal Ataturk is revered today throughout Turkey for the radical reforms he introduced during the 1920s and 30s. These included state education, industrialisation programs, and, most controversial of all, secularism. For 80 years, Islam in Turkey has been tightly controlled by the state. Ataturk's reforms have helped make Turkey the most economically successful Muslim country in the world. But they were achieved at a price. Ataturk was a soldier, and the military today has become the guardian of his principles, overthrowing democratically elected governments whenever these principles are threatened. And while secularism is hugely popular in Turkey itself, it is a source of continued political unrest. The recent spate of bombings in Istanbul are a tragic reminder that secular Turkey is a target for Islamic fundamentalists.[55]

Ataturk succeeded in liberal modernization by using nondemocratic methods. He suppressed the religious authority of clerics, separating mosque from state. Most of the mechanisms remain in place.[56] Ataturk, and the guardians of Turkish democracy today, recognized that modernity requires a secular government, and the role of religion is to provide moral guidance to the people, subordinate to secular law. Religion is not to rule. Americans should not allow an American value of religious freedom to confuse what leaders in the Islamic world know about their culture—theocracy is a threat.

As discussed earlier, there are conflicting ideologies with different worldviews confronting the United States. In constructing its desired future, the United States must develop the appropriate cultural savvy and apply it in the context of the society with which it is dealing. Islamic culture and the current GWOT illustrate what this may encompass and the broad concepts involved, but each culture confrontation will be somewhat unique.

DEALING WITH RADICAL OR RESURGING ISLAM:
AN ILLUSTRATIVE CASE

Radical Islam.

Of the three ideologies highlighted previously, Radical Islam is the most immediately threatening. A closer examination of the cultural implications on the GWOT can reveal insights into any confrontation. Most Americans, who consider themselves open-minded, fair, and balanced, are very uncomfortable dealing with Islam and all the intricacies of discerning radical ideology from true faith. The American self-image is one of a secular government promoting religious freedom, an element the more culturally savvy extremists have exploited. Radical Islamic extremists, ideological enemies of secularism and liberal democracy, hide their political and ideological aspirations behind a legitimate major world religion. This means Americans must learn how to deal with an issue in a manner that is politically incorrect by American standards. Clearly the American approach erred early as a result of a natural bias for freedom of religion. As suggested earlier, a better approach would have been to explore Islamic history and see how successful secular Islamic nations have dealt with Islam. Successful "apostate" Islamic nations have come to the conclusion that Islam must be addressed by promoting a separation of mosque and state. Such study also suggests this may be tougher than with other religions because of the Koran's focus on governance. Islam's guidance on just and moral government is radicalized easily by clerics. The challenge for U.S. policymakers and strategists becomes how to grapple with this issue in a constructive way — neither ignoring the threat nor attacking a world religion. To do this, they must first strive for strategic objectivity, avoiding the entanglements of both the U.S. culture and that of others. To recognize Islam as "different" goes against the American sense of equality and respect for religion or other diversity, yet such savvy provides the avenue for developing constructive strategic solutions — strategies that do not result in a clash of expectations.

On the other hand, American notions of universal commonalities or equality are challenged by psychological studies that show Muslims as a people are different. They do not share American values of individualism and personal freedom.

> The Geert Hofstede analysis for the Arab World that included the countries of Egypt, Iraq, Kuwait, Lebanon, Libya, Saudi Arabia, and the United Arab Emirates, demonstrates that the Muslim faith plays a significant role in people's lives. . . . The lowest Hofstede Dimension for the Arab World is the Individualism (DV) ranking at 38, compared to a world average ranking of 64. This translates into a Collectivist society as compared to an Individualist culture and is manifested in a close long-term commitment to the member group . . . Loyalty in a collectivist culture is paramount, and overrides most other societal rules.[57]

Again, the point here is that Americans must work hard to understand the nature of human cultural differences and reduce the clash of expectations. Western and Islamic culture and ideology differ on how to define modernity. Americans, on the forward edge of Western civilization, promote the advance of the individual over society and the creation of material wealth. Muslims, on the other hand, place more emphasis on spiritual wealth and the values of hierarchical traditional societies. Herein lies another cultural difference between the American and the traditional Islamic social model, which radicals can exploit easily by appealing to the collectivist nature of Islamic societies. The more Americans study Islam, the more they might conclude that the intricacies of promoting Western style reforms in Islamic cultures are best done through like-minded allies, at a pace and in a manner that promotes stability.

What most Americans find difficult to accept, because it is counterintuitive to our experience, is that radical Islam's success is proportional directly to Western lack of savvy in pulling the Islamic world into modernity. Western efforts to change the Islamic world, mostly lacking savvy and ignoring local sensitivities, have created radical opportunities by triggering populist waves of Islamic backlash trying to protect traditional societies from the extremes of western style values. So, the challenge for the United States becomes, essentially, how to convert Muslims to liberal capitalist modernity before extremists succeed in mobilizing an even greater number of people—both in Islamic countries and in the West—to their radical ideology to create Samuel Huntington's "clash of civilizations."[58] Such a clash may not occur on the battlefield but in the Western world, as evidenced by Muslims emigrating to the West carrying their way of life, while they are protected by the tenets of Western society until it is too late. The strategic question becomes, "How do we deal with the not yet guilty?"[59]

Islamic migration to Western Europe is a true test of wills between cultures. It is counterintuitive for Americans to think that Islamic gains in the Western world will be more lasting than Western secular promotion of democracy in the Islamic world. It is also counterintuitive to Western people—who cherish both the notions of freedom *of* religion and freedom *from* religion—that the spread of Islam among ethnic Western converts can be used by radicals to further the spread of radical Islamic ideology, directly countering Western notions of individual liberties and modernity. An example of this phenomenon can be seen in the Netherlands with Ms. Rabia's Frank's (formerly Rebecca Frank) conversion to Islam and public promotion of Islam through speech and wearing of the full Islamic body cover (hijab), in what is clearly a traditional Dutch secular society: "'What upsets people is that I am a Muslim first' . . . 'I am a Muslim,' she said with finality. 'That's my identity'."[60] Yet to respect Islam is to realize how strong a force for submission and social mobilization it is. In layman terms, it is a battle between "Western style liberation" versus traditional "submission" to God's law.

What the world is witnessing today is "Islamic populist manifest destiny" led by both individual and radical Muslims who take pride in their own culture, much to the chagrin of Western Europeans whose value sets they reject. Large numbers of Muslims fail to assimilate successfully in the West, highlighted by the London train and bus bombings which killed 51 in 2005 and were committed by British-born Muslims of Pakistani descent.[61] Islamic faith and radical ideology may well constitute stronger forces than secular Western allegiances, even among ethnic European converts. Islamic riots in France (November 2005) and the Danish cartoon incident (January-February 2006) are more recent illustrations of the strength of Islamic allegiance in Muslims in western societies and at home. Islamic majorities by the year 2050 in several European nations, such as Belgium and the Netherlands, are plausible, assuming current trends do not abate.[62] Henry Kissinger offers a perspective of this phenomenon:

> For the jihad phenomenon is more than the sum of individual terrorist acts extending from Bali through Jakarta, to New Delhi, Tunisia, Riyadh, Istanbul, Casablanca, Madrid, and London. It is an ideological outpouring comparable to the early days of Islam by which Islam's radical wing seeks to sweep away secularism, pluralistic values, and Western institutions wherever Muslims live. Its dynamism is fueled by the conviction that the designated victims are on the decline and lacking the will to resist. Any event that seems to confirm these convictions compounds the revolutionary dynamism.[63]

Unfortunately for Western liberalism, Islam's radicals promote an ideology that regards itself as superior to anything written by men. Simply put, these radicals confront Muslims at home and in Western countries with having to choose between God's law and man's law—and God's law is winning out.

> Radical Islamism is a byproduct of modernization itself, arising from the loss of identity that accompanies the transition to a modern, pluralist society. It is no accident that so many recent terrorists, from September 11 [2001]'s Mohamed Atta to the murderer of Dutch filmmaker Theo van Gogh to the London subway bombers, were radicalized in democratic Europe and intimately familiar with all of democracy's blessings. More democracy will mean more alienation, radicalization, and—yes, unfortunately—terrorism.[64]

The United States and the modern world need to reframe this question. To do this, the policymakers and strategists must develop cultural savvy and often do things that are counterintuitive to our own culture. It is intuitive for Americans to keep looking for a "reasonable" Islamic main-street and counterintuitive that the majority of Muslims see Islamic law as more reasonable than secular law. Many Americans prefer to believe that America is simply misunderstood, and the solution lies in reaching out better to the Islamic world. Americans, who believe this notion, are reaching for cultural commonalities and glossing over deep cultural differences that must be reconciled in pulling traditional Islamic societies into the modern world. As Lawrence correctly recognized in World War I: "We must also arrange the minds of the enemy so far as we could reach them . . . ."[65] The implications are clear. We must first understand that we can influence the mindset; and second, our ability to do so has limitations.

One key cultural difference between the West and Islamic peoples misunderstood by Westerners is the role of the *Koran*, the Islamic holy book, as civil law. In the United States, a very religious nation by western standards, religious law is adopted into civic law, where its merits can be debated and adjusted in a secular manner. Many Islamic nations have the *Koran* as an integral part of the civil law at different levels. This makes sense to a traditional culture in a non-Western region. Yet it means Islam, as a political ideology, promotes a theocracy with a rule of law more sacrosanct than the U.S. Constitution.

> Drawing a disrespectful cartoon of Mohammad is a grave offence under Shariah law . . . Islam does not accept the Western and Christian distinction between what is "objectively a sin," and what is "actually" one. For them, "ignorance of the law is no excuse," ever. Whereas we hold that in the eye of God, or even of a court, it might well be an excuse. Likewise, we recognize compulsion as an excuse; whereas, in the Islamic tradition, this is a nonstarter. That is why, to use an extreme case, a strict Shariah court might sentence a woman to death for adultery, who has been raped. For she, objectively, is an adulteress. The sentence might not seem fair, but that very "fairness" is a Western notion. A good Shariah judge is a "strict constructionist," like a good American Supreme Court judge. He cannot rewrite his Constitution. He can be merciful, however.[66]

What the Danish Cartoon incident of February 2006 highlights, even to the most idealistic person, is that the Islamic world value of protecting the image of the Prophet Mohammad exceeds the offensiveness of their own extremists' atrocities. This is a measure of the cultural gap. For radical Muslims, freedom of religion and principles of freedom of speech are meaningful only as tools to be used against the West. They are not traditional cultural imperatives as in the West.

The major challenge for the West in the Islamic world is to promote modernity without letting radicals outwit the West and turn the promotion into their own tool. Western rational explanation alone cannot do this in relations with cultures so different that even good intentions easily can be misconstrued as threats and where the cultural paradigm defies Western reason.

> When Muslims say you are not showing respect, I would say: you are not asking for my respect, you are asking for my submission," said Flemming Rose, the culture editor of *Jyllands-Posten*, the Danish newspaper that published the controversial Mohammad cartoons. In earlier periods of European history, NRC Handelsblad said, "a small religious dispute could lead to large- or small-scale wars. The Muslim immigration has thrown Europe back to the religious conflicts of the past.[67]

Handelsblad has it right. Europe's religious wars intertwined a transition to modernity with faith; rational explanation was debatable.

Islamic Allies.

Another difficult cultural element to consider is how to deal with Islamic allies, who themselves are walking a fine line in dealing with their own extremists. The United States needs to realize that the "reasonable" Muslims already in power are hanging on in places like Morocco, Tunisia, Egypt, Pakistan, and Turkey. Even traditional allies in seemingly stable Islamic countries such as Morocco are feeling extreme fundamentalist pressures from their populations. Morocco and other stable Islamic states are confronted with a new threat: radicals using democracy to destroy them from within.[68] As a result, representative government challenges the precepts of a modern state and the U.S. worldview. This line is even finer when the ruling class is also the protector of the faith.

Saudi Arabia, a key U.S. ally, has a strict Wahhabi Islamic population with a sworn duty to protect the holy sites of Mecca and Medina, and to promote Islam. "Wahhabi theology advocates a puritanical and legalistic stance in matters of faith and religious practice. Wahhabists see their role as a movement to restore Islam from what they perceive to be innovations, superstitions, deviances, heresies, and idolatries."[69] Wahhabis' faith takes precedence over the secular aspects of their lives. Yet, for Saudia Arabia's political leaders, it is clear that the nation's people must make the transformation into the modern world and realize the benefits largely exemplified by the western world, or their legitimacy is questioned and the government may fall. Both the national purpose and the people are immersed in Wahabism. The expectations are conflicting, and double standards abound internally and in Saudi relations with the West as a result of trying to meet all expectations. There is a certain amount of duplicity and paradox in balancing this. For example, while Saudi Wahhabist leaders encourage their citizens to promote Islam in the West, it remains a high crime to proselytize another faith in Saudi Arabia, in accordance with Sharia law. Saudi leaders seek an educated middle class, but women are required to conform to Islamic traditional dress. Buying Islamic oil has promoted a symbiotic trade relationship with Middle Eastern governments, with the unintended consequence of making it possible to finance the rise of Islamic fundamentalism. Individual Islamic citizens lavishly contribute to nongovernment organizations (NGOs) of dubious distinctions, financing the spread of extremist ideology and a radical way of life at home and in the West.[70] The resulting conflict is risking the leaders' own elite status and the modernization of their nations.[71] The leaders necessarily are duplicitous; for the short-term, their faith is intertwined with ideology and governance.

CENTERS OF GRAVITY

How should the United States confront such a threat to its worldview when the cultural differences are so great and the other culture also is conflicted internally? Again, a study of successful moderate Islamic regimes gives the United States starting points for relations with the Islamic world and clues as to the proper centers of gravity in the GWOT. Too often Americans look for physical centers of gravity. In the case of Islamic extremism, both enemy and friendly centers of gravity are more ideological or cultural than physical. To understand these centers of gravity, and how to get at them, requires cultural savvy. As Lawrence remands, success depends on being able to say: "The enemy I knew almost like my own side."[72] In the Islamic world, three centers of gravity stand out in the GWOT.

Leadership.

The first critical center of gravity is leadership. Islamic cultures are traditional and very hierarchical in nature. In such cultures, the leader is deferred to and largely obeyed as long as he has the legitimacy recognized by his traditional culture. The United States must support friendly, positive leadership and discredit negative and extremist leadership. Western nations can take four main areas of approach under the rubric of this center of gravity. These vulnerabilities can be addressed with specific objectives and concepts.

Under the leadership center of gravity, central to success is finding strong Islamic leaders who can both work with the United States to further national objectives and have the credibility to work with their own people. By using strong Islamic leaders, one exploits the vulnerability in that such collective societies support their own legitimate rulers. Such a leader must have the stature to maintain the respect of tribal elders, warlords, clerics, and the people at large. With this respect, the leader controls sufficient forces to regain control of rogue elements within his borders. Ideally, such a leader would be Western educated and have the savvy to engineer a complex hybrid of Western democratic egalitarianism with a local brand of democracy, under the rule of secular law. Like-minded allies are much better at communicating with their own people and enjoy, as a general rule, cultural trust. American cultural biases are so ingrained that they will always be a factor. Hence, the United States should seek to minimize the physical contact between its forces and the foreign public as much as possible in culturally distinct places as the Middle East and Asia. The smarter concept is to encourage and support people who will work positively with the United States. The payoffs from such an approach could be incredible through an immediate reduction of cultural clashes. No better press exists than a foreign leader explaining America's positive virtues, as we have witnessed with President Musharraf of Pakistan.[73] America's energies are better used indirectly in promoting ideas, programs, and leaders whose collective efforts lead over time to the world the United States envisions.

A second avenue under the leadership center of gravity is to invite Islamic clerics and tribal elders to work with you, recognizing them as a vulnerability. Islam fosters traditional hierarchical social networks. The highest form of respect an outsider can demonstrate is to recognize both formal and informal social and religious networks. In such traditional societies, it is much more efficient to work with these existing leaders than it is to bypass them, intentionally or not.[74] Cultural savvy allows one to recognize the relative power tribal elders and clerics have over their communities. A given foreign presence explained to the people by their own leaders normally provides more appeal, credibility, and legitimacy than if a foreigner attempts to communicate directly with the masses. As such, every effort should be made to work with these leaders, rather than ignore them. Moderate Islamic clerics, in particular, should be seen as having a significant impact on the local national Islamic population and can be an invaluable ally in motivating the local population to reject extremism. Their critical positions in the Islamic faith and their ability to help isolate radical clerics and extremists make them key allies.

A third avenue under the leadership center of gravity is that the United States and its allies must be willing to keep targeting radical extremist leaders with kinetic means. They are a vulnerability because extremist behavior is viewed as abnormal in a collectivist society where people look for the common good. It is common sense to target and neutralize radical extremists using the full spectrum of legitimate powers available to the state, given they will not compromise with the West. Islamic culture respects strength and radicals do not lend themselves to compromising on principle. However, cultural savvy should cause pause to understand the impact of inflicting casualties and ensuing blood feuds that should be avoided:

> "An eye for an eye" or the current Arab saying, "Dam butlab dam" ("Blood demands blood") . . . The blood feud is an organic part and inevitable consequence of the intensive group cohesion which characterizes the Arab ethos. A society in which great emphasis is placed on the kin group, in which the individual interests are subordinated to the interests of family and lineage, and in which, in addition, honor is given the highest priority, it is inevitable that every homicide, premeditated or accidental, should give rise to blood revenge and trigger a chain reaction that soon involves an increasing number of men and groups . . . Just as the taking of blood revenge was considered a value and redounded to one's honor, so was fighting in general.[75]

A fourth avenue under the leadership center of gravity is ultimately the Turkish model of reducing Islamic cleric influence in politics through the promotion of separation of "Mosque and State." Islam's call for just governance is a vulnerability. Separation of mosque and state is difficult to sustain due to the unique cultural role of Islam in governance. Even secular Turkey is dealing with a resurgence of Islamism that is walking a fine line between promoting Turkish nationalism and joining Pan-Islamic radicalism.[76] It sometimes requires nondemocratic actions such as "when the Islamist Prime Minister Necemettin Erbakan took power in 1996, the Turkish military, which regards itself as the ultimate guardian of the secularist democratic tradition of modern Turkey . . . elegantly eased Erbakan out of power."[77] Secular leadership must be built throughout a society, and such leaders must be willing to take steps to outmaneuver clerics and radical populists with creative local solutions that provide obvious, just, and advantageous governance. The influence of clerics, and with it Islam, must be reduced for nations to continue with modernity since "Muslims tend to reject the Western concept of man creating his own environment as an intrusion on God's realm. This includes any attempt to change God's plan for the fate of the individual."[78] Yet, successful governance by a religious secular leader can separate mosque and state.

Communications.

Another critical center of gravity is communications since both the United States and the extremists depend on effective use of the media. Two areas where savvy and objectivity must be applied are Information Operations (IO) and U.S. public diplomacy.[79] It seems intuitive to Americans that the West can do a better job of communicating with the Islamic world than extremists. It is counterintuitive that the Islamic world may not wish to hear the Western message, given ample Islamic domestic press and web sites. The vulnerability is the Islamic public's sources of information. In a sense, Islamic extremists are using the Islamic media and the Internet as their vehicles to promote a return to the 9th century. From a culturally savvy point of view, there are two main avenues for the United States to pursue.

First is to get friendly or willing allied Islamic governments to promote the United States as a partner that is allied with the Islamic world against extremism. Governments in the Islamic world generally control the public media resources. U.S. public diplomacy, standing on its merit, is not effective. Friendly nations, such as the United Arab Emirates (UAE), Afghanistan, Pakistan, Jordan, Turkey, Tunisia, Egypt, Malaysia, and Indonesia, could be invaluable if they shifted from a public position of silence or playing to the street to promoting the United States actively in the Islamic world in the local language. Until friendly Islamic governments assist the United States in its public diplomacy challenge, the Islamic main-street will perceive the United States to be an unwelcome guest in the Islamic world. For example,

> following the September 11, 2001, terrorist attacks in the United States, Musharraf sided with the United States against the Taliban government in Afghanistan. Musharraf agreed to give the United States the use of three airbases for Operation ENDURING FREEDOM. Secretary of State Colin Powell and other administration officials met with Musharraf. Musharraf's reversal of policy and help to the U.S. military was critical in the U.S. bombing that rapidly overcame the Taliban regime.[80]

Islamic public media will be more objective in its coverage, if the government demands it.

Second is to manipulate directly or shut down radical extremist web sites and Internet communications. Radical Islam is a true global insurgency with the goal of promoting the spread of extremism and "winning the hearts and minds" of undecided Muslims. Islamic extremists are effective at using the Internet for command and control and for actively promoting war against the United States and the West. The United States must act decisively in this area. Such decisive action must include changing U.S. law as needed. Radical extremist web sites must be dealt with in a similar manner to enemy radio communications during past wars. To make any distinctions between traditional radio electronic combat and web sites based on freedom of the press arguments is to cede the initiative to an enemy equally, if not more, sophisticated than the United States and its western allies.

Islamic Women.

The third—and most critical center of gravity in the Islamic world—is the *role of Islamic women* and prospects for their *liberation*. Women in the Islamic world are second class citizens, codified by the Koran and reinforced by prevailing "Arab male attitudes to women: that the destiny of women, in general, and in particular of those within the family circle, is to serve the men and obey them."[81] Women's rights are a critical vulnerability. Long-term success in the field of women's rights in most of the Islamic world, however, will require significant societal reforms. If Islamic women truly receive full civil protection and equality, it will lead to secular law. In layman's terms, free the women, and you have a chance at neutralizing the males who apply scripture literally in the 9th century sense. Liberation or equal rights for women could even trigger a "reformation" in the Islamic world to temper extremism and radicalism, reducing radical ideology to an insignificant role. Sharia, in contrast, codifies total submission of the individual to Islamic society.[82] Under the banner of women's rights, other societal reforms can usher in other pillars of democracy: minority rights, due process of law, freedom of speech, freedom of minority religions, property rights, and a judicial process to address grievances under due process of secular law. Without supporting societal reforms, terrorist organizations, like Hamas, thrive in democracy, furthering the unfortunate prospects of "one man, one vote, one time" in a radicalized society.[83]

Applying "cultural savvy," the United States can see with strategic objectivity, knowing when to act directly and when to hide its hand behind the scenes with allies. In the true Clausewitzian spirit of "War is merely the continuation of policy by other means, the United States must focus on end-state and recognize that in GWOT the centers of gravity are more cultural than physical."[84] Simply said, U.S. leaders must learn to be more "Machiavellian" in their relationships and planning in regard to other cultures. The United States must think counterintuitively and look for indirect, and perhaps, advantageous multilateral arrangements to obtain its end. These approaches ultimately lead to success, but often are built on the foundations of effective U.S. military operations.

IMPLICATIONS FOR THE MILITARY:
EDUCATION AND TRAINING

Within the military, the keys to properly understanding centers of gravity and getting at the vulnerabilities with supporting concepts of military operations are cultural education and training and foreign language training, all of which serve to provide the grounds for working better with allies in a more mutually symbiotic way. True reform in the way Americans deal with foreign cultures is best served through long-term and sustained education, preferably learned through foreign contact before entering the military. This is a long-term strategic imperative for the nation, but the military must confront the challenge today.

The U.S. military is engaged actively in the field around the world. Soldiers in the field can embarrass the United States when they make a cultural mistake, with immediate world-wide visibility in this age of mass media and instant communications. Often, such embarrassments have strategic consequences. Soldiers may never be made perfect diplomats, but they can be educated and trained to avoid egregious cultural blunders. Every soldier needs to understand the strategic public affairs message of both the United States and the enemy, and his role in regard to them. This is the clear lesson of the Abu Ghraib prison scandal, the Guantanamo Bay detainee allegations, and the incident in Afghanistan in 2005, as captured by an Australian cameraman related to the burning of alleged Taliban bodies.[85] Every U.S. serviceman is capable of having a tactical action escalate to the strategic level. So, cross-cultural training is essential, yet there are challenges: "While these programs have proven useful, they fall short of generating the understanding necessary for today's complex settings, especially when values and norms are so divergent, they clash."[86] The military must develop effective education and training for all soldiers and their leaders.

Training.

A significant challenge for the military is to shift its view on "cultural training" from one which restrains Americans to one that empowers them. Often cultural education or training is confused for sensitivity or diversity training when it should be promoted as cultural effectiveness training. Again, a fine and nuanced balance exists between being culturally sensitive and being effective. A "street-smart" soldier, at any level, demonstrates the necessary leadership acumen to get a culturally distinct foreign national to support what he needs to do. A pitfall of "cultural training" is confusing internal U.S. diversity training with the essential knowledge required by U.S. personnel for effective foreign interactions. If "cultural training" is done correctly, one will develop a reasonable understanding of a given culture for the purpose of finding common ground to focus better on what is necessary for mission success.

> In fact, engagement with local populations has become so crucial that mission success often is affected significantly by a soldier's ability to interact with local individuals and communities. Learning to interact with local populaces presents a major challenge for soldiers, leaders and civilians.[87]

Too often, teaching culture is boiled down into the prism of simplistic "do's and don'ts that is expected to allow the service-member to leap the cultural gap."[88] The gap is more than this. Americans automatically should not dismiss or discount information which might seem like stereotyping, or contrary to what is considered politically correct by American culture. To be savvy culturally, Americans need a better understanding of the differences between themselves and the foreign nationals they seek to deal with, and bridge cultural gaps based on an objective assessment of risk and gain. Others stereotype Americans. The following simplistic biases are commonly at work as bonds are formed: Americans are monolingual and fit a loud and obnoxious cowboy image. As such, often this is the first stereotype the American falls into in the first series of encounters, given that his counterpart has to make the effort to speak in English to the American, with all the associated customs that come with that. As a general rule, Americans are seen as proud of anti-intellectualism as clearly depicted in countless Hollywood action movies where the street-wise American punk outwits either the European or Asian elite "bad guys." "For Americans, history is bunk."[89] When Americans gloat of their cultural ignorance of geography, history (both their own and world history), science, and mathematics, they are living up to a popular stereotype. The world is metric, and they are not. Sports talk is generally an excellent means of building relationships. Yet, American's generally play sports developed in North America: baseball, basketball, and American football—not soccer. Americans prefer "chain restaurants" and food with national commercial recognition. While this seems like a trivial distinction, it is one not lost on foreign counterparts who believe diet can denote socio-economic status. To an American, a "chain restaurant" denotes modernity. Cultural savvy requires a deeper level of education, one that allows Americans to make useful distinctions in stereotypes and mitigate negative stereotypes of Americans.

Training is more short-term focused and generally provided in response to an upcoming task and deployment. Today, the U.S. military has a very short-term focus on cultural training, which poorly postures the force for an ever increasingly "globalized" world. In the short-term, troops will better respond to cultural training if they get better "politically *in*correct" training which actually provides a tangible tactical field advantage—telling them how it really is so they can build workable cultural bridges.

Education.

As a part of transformation, foreign language proficiency needs to be a skill prized and rewarded by financial incentives in the military, as it is with the U.S. Department of State. A short-term U.S. military solution would be to offer all service members, regardless of rank, duty position, or specialty, financial incentives that reward self-study in any number of languages of their choosing. Financial incentives should reward even the most rudimentary capabilities which could be administered on-line through Service education centers, perhaps twice a year, and linked to a Department of Defense (DoD) database for the purposes of pay and linguist availability for contingencies—without the bureaucratic and limited nature of the current Foreign Language Proficiency Pay (FLPP) system, which is inadequate.[90] There is no substitute for leveraging local knowledge and "hiding one's hand" in the political-military interface with a traditional culture: skills that depend on mastery of the local language. The U.S. military must make attracting linguists a major strategic priority as part of a paradigm shift if we are to reduce needless friction and enjoy greater success.

Another critical cultural education task is the art of negotiations. In cultural confrontations, every step forward is the result of negotiation. Since there are always differing purposes and agendas, soldiers need to keep in mind how to protect U.S. positions, while figuring out what can be reasonably bartered in the process. All negotiation is based on knowledge and skills—acquired attributes. American "legitimacy" is on the table in every negotiation. Americans like the image of being "straight shooters in a duplicitous world." Face-to-face negotiations with foreign counterparts is an area where one sees the most obvious challenges for Americans. Americans erode a "starting position" with thoughts of compromise before understanding the cultural dynamics at work. Americans will take another's word if they "look 'em in the eye" and impress them as being honorable. Americans want to believe Muslims who say their faith is tolerant and being hijacked by radicals. Yet, duplicity may be a tool to beguile "infidels" into letting their guard down. Negotiations education can level the playing field by explaining the roles and providing the strategies for success. Again, it is counterintuitive for Americans to work indirectly in any manner which might appear to be Machiavellian or that works at a slower pace than direct action. What American culture fails to appreciate is that the shortest distance between two positions may be cultural savvy.

Foreign language education is the long-term solution to U.S. cultural woes with the world, since language is the key for understanding critical nuances of culture. Language education and training is essential for Americans to understand their foreign counterparts. A compounding problem is the lack of elementary school foreign language education in the United States. More often than not, foreign language instruction in the United States is not considered yet a "core curriculum" course at the elementary school level.[91] An abundance of literature supports foreign language education during early child development. It is ironic that America has pushed trade globalization to promote world prosperity, and yet does not recognize the need to transform its education system to prepare tomorrow's business leaders to take advantage of the opportunities. However, one should not expect even the best language and culture training to be a panacea that can substitute for years of experience. Consider the experience of the senior U.S. Commander in the Republic of Korea (ROK) in 1979, General John A. Wickham:

> My shallow linguistic ability, however, did not lend me a deep understanding of the culture. For that, I had to turn to my valuable assistants, Steve Bradner, who had married a Korean Olympic athlete, and Bruce Grant, who was fluent in Korean and Chinese. They had spent much of their adult lives in Korea, and Bruce was author of several books on Korean culture.[92]

Up to here, the point has been made that contrary to the notion of American idealism or exceptionalism, people around the world are indeed different and that is why cultural knowledge matters. With this said, while no one can realistically suppress all cultural biases, we can mitigate them by thinking counterintuitively. "Deal(ing) with the world as it is . . . not as we wish it were"[93] requires curbing domestic intuitions with very precise cultural knowledge in order to discern the seen and unseen, and acting appropriately in regard to both. Education combined with experience will develop soldiers and leaders who are culturally savvy.

CONCLUSION

History reveals that few states have risen to dominate their epoch, and no nation has been able to maintain dominance forever. Unlike past states, the United States does not seek to rule directly but to create a world order in which it can prosper with its values intact. Yet, as a western power, the United States cannot overlook the fact that the majority of the world's population no longer wants direct pejorative leadership from the "white man." Americans need to think counterintuitively to their own culture to find successful long-term strategies for creating a better world. Such strategies must avoid mirror imaging, the trap of seeking commonalities, and idealistic wishful thinking. Given its relative minority status, the United States needs to apply more cultural savvy, working in the world as it is in order to build the world it desires. America has worthy goals in promoting democracy and free trade, but needs to figure out how to better pursue them more indirectly, through like-minded allies. Never before have the following words been more relevant advice for U.S. policymakers who need to identify how to sustain American leadership and promote core values, while addressing root causes of anti-Americanism clearly gaining momentum today: "Better to let them do it imperfectly than to do it perfectly yourself, for it is their country, their way, and our time is short."[94]

Cultural savvy, for the sake of it, is simply not compelling to the pragmatist, unless it provides tangible results. In today's world, pragmatic reasons to promote cultural savvy can be found in the hard reality of addressing why U.S. leadership is being challenged by friend and foe alike. There is real need for introspection in how to adapt and overcome this "push back." Better cultural savvy also is needed to reconcile the American view of the world with the rise of competing foreign ideologies. The existence of pragmatic non-Western ideological alternatives seems lost on American leadership. While this paper focused on the mobilization of extremist Islam against the West as a case study, the United States must not be so myopic as to miss the level of anti-Americanism around the world, and how other alternative ideologies are on the march. With improved cultural savvy, it is possible for a more objective assessment of what America is in relation to the world, and adopt strategies which will promote the U.S. worldview. Cultural education and training must be shifted from techniques that restrain Americans to knowledge and methods that empower them. Unless the United States grasps and applies this strategic truth, it will not be able to sustain its positive balance of economic, political, socio-psychological, and military power in the global community.

ENDNOTES

1. Douglas J. Feith, "Transformation and Security Cooperation," September 8, 2004; linked from DoD Homepage at *www.defenselink.mil/speeches/2004/sp20040908-0722.html*, Internet, accessed March 14, 2006. Douglas J. Feith was the Under Secretary of Defense for Policy; speech at the COMDEF 2004 Conference, National Press Club, Washington, DC.

2. Bernard Henri Levy, "American Vertigo, Traveling America in the Footsteps of Tocqueville," interview on live national television by Fox News, March 6, 2006/1745hrs EST.

3. Reem Al-Faisal, "Can a Value System Supposedly Primitive Pose a Threat to the West?" *Arab News,* March 14, 2006, [newspaper on line], available from *www.arabview.com/articles.asp?article=588*, Internet, accessed March 15, 2006.

4. James Kurth, "The American Way of Victory," *The National Interest,* Summer 2000 [journal on-line], available from *www.ciaonet.org/olj/ni/ni_00kuj01.html*, Internet, accessed March 15, 2006, p. 185.

5. Colonel T. E. Lawrence, as referenced by Lieutenant Colonel William Wunderle, "Through the Lens of Cultural Awareness; Planning Requirements in Wielding the Instruments of National Power," in a Microsoft Power Point presentation with scripted commentary, April 21, 2005, slide 15. Lieutenant Colonel William Wunderle is a U.S. Army Infantry officer and Middle East Foreign Area Officer (FAO) serving as Senior Army Research Fellow, RAND Corporation.

6. Feith.

7. George W. Bush, *National Security Strategy of the United States*, Washington, DC: The White House, September 2002, p. 1.

8. George W. Bush, address to the American Legion, Washington, DC, February 28, 2006, broadcast on CSPAN television.

9. George W. Bush, as referenced by Rear Admiral Bill Sullivan, "Fighting the Long War—Military Strategy for the War on Terrorism," Microsoft Power Point presentation with scripted commentary, presented to the Executive Lecture Forum, Radvanyi Chair in International Security Studies, Mississippi State University, October 6, 2005, slide 19. Rear Admiral Sullivan is the Vice Director for Strategic Plans and Policy, The Joint Staff, Washington, DC.

10. *Ibid.*, slide 8.

11. Sun Tzu, *The Art of War*, Samuel Griffith, trans., New York, NY: Oxford University Press, 1963, p. 84.

12. Bush, as referenced by Sullivan, slide 8.

13. Francis Fukuyama, "Europe vs. Radical Islam; Alarmist Americans Have Mostly Bad Advice for Europe," *Slate*, February 27, 2006 [newspaper on-line], available from *www.slate.com/id/2136964/?nav=tap3*, Internet, accessed March 15, 2006.

14. Bush, *National Security Strategy*, p. 1.

15. Barbara Slavin, "Mideast Democracy Boots Islamists," *USA Today*, January 25, 2006, Front Page.

16. Bill Schneider, "Lou Dobbs Tonight," interview on live national television on CNN, October 11, 2005, 1838hrs EST.

17. Henry Kissinger, "China Shifts Centre of Gravity," *The Australian*, June 13, 2005 [newspaper on-line], available from *www.taiwansecurity.org/news/2005/AS-130605.htm*, Internet, accessed March 1, 2006.

18. Jackson Diehl, "A Losing Latin Policy," *The Washington Post*, March 10, 2006 [newspaper on line], available from *www.washingtonpost.com/wp-dyn/content/linkset/2005/03/24/LI2005032401551.html*, Internet, accessed March 14, 2006.

19. Monte Reel, "Bolivian Nods to Indian Roots," *The Washington Post*, January 22 2006, sec. A, p. A18.

20. Diehl.

21. *Wikipedia*, The Free Encyclopedia, "Mar del Plata Summit of the Americas," February 16, 2006 [reference on-line], available from *en.wikipedia.org/wiki/Mar_del_Plata_Summit_of_the_Americas*, Internet, accessed March 2, 2006.

22. Trudy Morales, "The Evo Morales Factor and Indigenous Resurgence in Bolivia: What is Ahead for U.S.-Bolivia Relations?" lecture, Dickinson College, Carlisle, PA, March 1, 2006.

23. Dr. Gabriel Marcella, e-mail message to author, January 9, 2006, 0918hrs. Dr. Marcella is a U.S. Army War College professor from the Department of National Strategic Studies, Carlisle Barracks, PA. Point of view was in reference to the following article forwarded by another War College professor, Dr. Louis J. Nigro, Jr., Professor of International Relations: Peter Hakim, "Is Washington Losing Latin America?" *Foreign Affairs*, January/February 2006 [journal on-line], available from *www.foreignaffairs.org/ 20060101faessay85105/peter-hakim/is-washington-losing-latin-america.html*, Internet, accessed January 4, 2006.

24. Al-Faisal.

25. Levy.

26. Joseph Farah, "Islam on March South of Border, Mexico Agrees to Monitor Foreign Groups as Muslim Recruitment Rate Skyrockets," *The World Net Daily*, June 7, 2005 [newspaper on line], available from *www.worldnetdaily.com/news/article.asp?ARTICLE_ID=44636*, Internet, accessed March 14, 2006.

27. Phillip K. Abbot, "Terrorist Threat in the Tri-Border Area: Myth or Reality?" September-October 2004, The U.S. Army Homepage, available from *www.army.mil/professionalwriting/volumes/volume3/january_2005/1_05_4.html*, Internet, accessed March 14, 2006.

28. Dana Harman, "FBI Confronts New Gang Threat," February 24, 2005, *The Christian Science Monitor* [newspaper on-line], available from *www.christiansciencemonitor.com/2005/0224/p01s02-woam.html*, Internet, accessed March 15, 2006.

29. Robert Cooper, *The Breaking of Nations, Order and Chaos in the Twenty First Century*, New York, NY: Atlantic Monthly Press, 2003, p. 16.

30. *Ibid.*, pp. 44-49.

31. Colonel Susan A. Browning, *Understanding Non-Western Cultures: A Strategic Intelligence Perspective,* Strategy Research Project, Carlisle Barracks, PA: U.S. Army War College, April 9, 1997, p. 8.

32. Richard D. Lewis, *When Cultures Collide, Managing Successfully Across Cultures*, London, UK: Nicholas Brealey Publishing, 1999, p. 30.

33. This joke was told at the U.S. Military Delegation to the NATO Military Committee Christmas Party, December 2005, in mixed company, and without intending insult, by a Slovakian Intelligence and Operations Planner/representative to NATO at an official function, in the presence of fellow colleagues from at least seven nations, to the roar of laughter, but with no malice intended. The author quickly was defended by his French Operations counterpart, Captain Christian Canova, of the French Navy.

34. Edward Trimnell, "Why You Need a Foreign Language, Edward Trimnell on the Myth of Global English and the Costs of Americans' Monolingualism," *Transition Abroad Magazine,* May-June 2005 [magazine on-line], available from *www. transitionsabroad.com/publications/magazine/0505/edward_trimnell_on_language_immersion.shtml*, Internet, accessed March 14, 2006.

35. Don Snider, "The Future of the Army Profession," Chapter 28, in *Strategic Leadership of the Army Profession,* 2d ed., Lloyd Matthews, Leonard Wong, and Don M. Snider, eds., New York, NY: McGraw-Hill, 2005, p. 615.

36. Colin S. Gray, "Strategy in the Nuclear Age: The United States, 1945-1991," *The Making of Strategy: Rulers, States and War,* Williamson Murray, Macgregor Knox, and Alvin Berstein, eds., New York: Cambridge University Press, 1994, p. 588.

37. USFK J3, "Counterpart Guide to Korea," August 2000, available from USFK J3 homepage */www.korea.army.mil/org/j3/ ed/korea/communicate2.html*, Internet; accessed January 28, 2006, p. 22.

38. *Ibid.*

39. Mike Shuster, "North Korea, Iran Watching U.S. Nuclear Tactics," *National Public Radio,* March 15, 2006 [news on-line], available from *www.npr.org/templates/story/story.php?storyId=5072690*, Internet, accessed March 15, 2006.

40. MSNBC News Services, "Three-pronged Approach Comes While IAEA Discusses Nuclear Program," MSNBC News Services, March 7, 2007 [newspaper online], available from *www.msnbc.msn.com/id/11681845/*, Internet, accessed March 13, 2006.

41. Paul Marshall, "Taliban Light, Afghanistan Fast Forwards," *National Review Online,* November 7, 2003 [journal on-line], available from *www.nationalreview.com/comment/marshall200311070906.asp*, Internet, accessed March 15, 2006.

42. *Ibid.* Paul Marshall is senior fellow at Freedom House's Center for Religious Freedom. He is reachable through *www. benadorassociates.com.*

43. James Fallows, "Blind into Baghdad," *The Atlantic Monthly*, January/February 2004, p. 6; also available from *www. theatlantic.com/doc/prem/200401/fallows*, Internet, accessed March 14, 2006.

44. Sun Tzu, p. 77.

45. Lewis, p. 30; Joe Klein, "Saddam's Revenge," *Time Magazine,* September 26, 2005, pp. 47-48.

46. Katherine Shrader, "U.S. Zarqawi's Terror Network Growing," *Comcast Homepage*, October 22, 2005 [news on-line], available from *www.comcast.net/news/index.jsp?cat=GENERAL&fn=/2005/10/22/247835.html*, Internet, accessed October 24, 2005.

47. Eliot A. Cohen, "Will We Persevere," *Wall Street Journal,* February 24, 2006, sec. A, p. A13.

48. Carl Von Clausewitz, *On War*, Michael Howard and Peter Paret, eds. and trans., Princeton, NJ: Princeton University Press, 1976, p. 90.

49. Mortimer B. Zuckerman, "In No Uncertain Terms," *U.S. News and World Report*, March 20, 2006, p. 72.

50. Lieutenant Colonel John A. Nagl, *Counterinsurgence Lessons Learned from Malaya and Vietnam, Eating Soup with a Knife,* Westport, CT: Prager, 2002. Taken from an announcement flyer for the Perspectives in Military History, *38th Annual Seminar Series,* October 19, 2005, entitled *"Can We Eat Soup with a Knife? Counterinsurgency Lessons from Vietnam and Iraq."*

51. Lecture, U.S. Army War College, Carlisle Barracks, PA, 2005. Lecturer was a senior officer covered by the U.S. Army War College "non-attribution" policy as part of its distinguished lecture series.

52. Paul Kennedy, "Why Did the British Empire Last So Long?" in *Strategy and Diplomacy, 1870-1945: Eight Studies,* London, UK: Polity Press, 1983, p. 208.

53. British Officer, famous line from the movie, *Last of the Mohicans*, Twentieth Century Fox Entertainment, Inc., Beverly Hills, CA, Box 900, 90213-0900, 1999, available from *www.stationfive.com/movies/Scripts/Last_of_the_Mohicans_The.txt*, Internet, accessed March 13, 2006.

54. Kennedy, p. 209.

55. The Europeans Radio National, "Attaturk's Legacy. Part 1: A Universal Civilisation," November 30, 2003, available from *www.abc.net.au/rn/talks/europe/stories/s1006506.htm*, Internet, accessed March 13, 2006.

56. Yusuf Kanli, "Frustrated and Confused," *Turkish Daily* News, *Liberal*, September 30, 2006 [newspaper on-line], available from *www.worldpress.org/Europe/2155.cfm* under "Turkey and the European Union" section, Internet, accessed on March 7, 2006.

57. Randy Borum, *Psychology of Terrorism*, Tampa, FL: University of South Florida, 2004, p. 44.

58. Samuel P. Huntington, "The Clash of Civilizations?" *Foreign Affairs*, Summer 1993 [journal on-line], available from *www.foreignaffairs.org/19930601faessay5188/samuel-p-huntington/the-clash-of-civilizations.html*, Internet, accessed March 15, 2006.

59. Lieutenant General Timothy Kinnan, USAF. Question he raised at the U.S. Military Delegation to the NATO Military Committee during the course of a Western European terrorism update, March 4, 2004.

60. Molly Moore, "Dutch Convert to Islam: Veiled and Viewed as a Traitor," *The Washington Post*, March 19, 2006, sec. A, p. A21.

61. BBC News, "London Bombers Were All British," *BBC News*, July 12, 2005 [newspaper on-line], available from *news. bbc.co.uk/1/hi/uk/4676577.stm*, Internet, accessed March 14, 2006.

62. Euro-Islam Info, "Country Profiles: Belgian Demographics," *Euro-Islam.Info*, March 2006 [resource on-line], available from *euro-islam.info/pages/belgium.html*, Internet, accessed March 14, 2006.

63. Henry A. Kissinger, "Moving Toward a Responsible Exit Strategy in Iraq," *San Diego Union Tribune*, December 11, 2005 [newspaper on-line], available from *www.signonsandiego.com/uniontrib/20051211/news_1e11kissn.html*, Internet, accessed December 14, 2005.

64. Francis Fukuyama, "After Neo-conservatism," *The New York Times*, February 19, 2006 [newspaper on-line], available from *zfacts.com/p/236.html*, Internet, accessed March 13, 2006.

65. Colonel T. E. Lawrence, from the book "Seven Pillars of Wisdom," as referenced by Lieutenant Colonel (R) Gregg Wilcox, "On Losing the Information War," in a Microsoft Power Point presentation of the U.S. Army War College with scripted commentary, slide 3.

66. David Warren, "Incompatibilities," *Ottawa Citizen*, February 13, 2006 [newspaper on-line], available from *www. realclearpolitics.com/Commentary/com-2_13_06_DW.html*, Internet, accessed February 13, 2006.

67. Alan Cowell, "A 'dangerous moment' for Europe and Islam," *The New York Times*, February 7, 2006 [newspaper on-line], available from *www.iht.com/articles/2006/02/07/news/europe.php*, Internet, accessed March 13, 2006.

68. Craig Whitlock, "Feud with the King Tests Freedoms in Morocco," *The Washington Post*, February 12, 2006, sec. A, p. A1.

69. *Wikipedia*, The Free Encyclopedia, "Wahhabism," February 16, 2006 [reference on-line], available from *en.wikipedia. org/wiki/Wahhabism*, Internet, accessed March 7, 2006.

70. Moustafa Osman, "Muslim NGOs Can Help Bridge Culture Gap," *Global Policy*, January 24, 2003 [newspaper on-line], available from *www.globalpolicy.org/ngos/aid/2003/0124muslim.htm*, Internet, accessed March 7, 2006. Islamic charities sometimes are accused of favoring their own people or trying to convert unbelievers. Moustafa Osman, program manager of Islamic Relief, explains why such criticism is unfair and argues that Muslim NGOs have a special role to play in peacekeeping and fundraising for humanitarian projects. This article first appeared in *Humanitarian Affairs Review*.

71. *Ibid*. Wahhabism, (Wahabism, Wahabbism) is a Sunni fundamentalist Islamic movement named after Muhammad ibn Abd al Wahhab (1703-92). It is the dominant form of Islam in Saudi Arabia and Qatar.

72. Colonel T. E. Lawrence, as referenced by Wunderle, slide 15.

73. Muzi, "Bush, Musharraf Renew Anti-Terror Alliance," *Muzi.com*, March 5, 2006 [newspaper on-line], available from *latelinenews.com/news/ll/english/10004891.shtml?cc=23534&ccr=*, Internet, accessed March 13, 2006.

74. Raphael Patai, *The Arab Mind*, New York, NY: Hatherleigh Press, 2002, pp. 83-88.

75. *Ibid.*, pp. 221-222.

76. Efraim Inbar, "Turkey's Election and Israel," *Jerusalem Center for Public Affairs*, December 30, 2002 [journal on-line], available from *www.jcpa.org/brief/brief2-15.htm*, Internet, accessed March 14, 2006.

77. *Ibid*.

78. Patai, p. xvi.

79. *The United States Department of State Home Page*, available from *www.state.gov/r/us/16269.htm*, Internet, accessed March 13, 2006. Sometimes even the best public relations effort does not improve a person's or an institution's image. Think of the U.S. State Department's $15 million "Shared Values" ad campaign, which tried to assuage anti-American sentiment in Muslim countries. "Shared Values" was a public relations campaign organized by the U.S. State Department to combat anti-American sentiment in Arab countries. The campaign used television advertising, speaking tours, town-hall meetings, print publications, radio broadcasts, and Arab outreach programs. Charlotte Beers, a former advertising executive who became U.S. undersecretary for public diplomacy after September 11, 2001, was the driving force behind Shared Values. One of its first public initiatives was a $15 million advertising campaign that broadcast TV spots in several Arab countries. The ads, which attempted to ease anti-American sentiment by featuring Muslim Americans talking about their positive experiences living in the United States, began broadcasting in December 2002. However, they were discontinued after only a month. A State Department spokesman denied that the advertising campaign was a failure. "Those spots were only intended to run during the month of Ramadan, and they were completed successfully on schedule," he said. In June 2003, however, the U.S. State Department launched an inquiry into the failure of Shared Values to polish America's image in Muslim countries after an opinion poll conducted by the Pew Research Center for the People and the Press found that that negative views of the United States were on the rise in the Middle East.

80. *Wikipedia*, The Free Encyclopedia, "Pervez Musharaf, After September 11, 2001," available from *en.wikipedia.org/wiki/Pervez_Musharaf*, Internet, accessed March 14, 2006.

81. Patai, p. 34.

82. Warren.

83. Michael Rubin, "To Islamists, One Man, One Vote, One Time Means Dictatorship," *The Daily Star*, June 7, 2005 [newspaper on-line], available from *www.dailystar.com.lb/article.asp?edition_id=10&categ_id=5&article_id=15704*, Internet, accessed March 14, 2006.

84. Clausewitz, p. 87.

85. Stephen Dupont, "Afghanistan Update," CBS television news footage rebroadcast by CNN and interview on live national television by CNN, October 20 2005, 1455hrs EST.

86. McFarland, pp. 131-133.

87. *Ibid.*

88. *Ibid.*

89. Cooper, p. 48.

90. *Military.com*, "Foreign Language Proficiency Pay (FLPP)," [reference on-line], available from *www.military.com/Resources/ResourceFileView/Pay_Officers_Foreign.htm-5k-*, Internet, accessed on March 15, 2006. A reform of the FLPP program went into effect April 1, 2000. The primary focus of the reformed FLPP program is to act as an incentive for military members in career linguist occupations to increase their foreign language proficiency. FLPP-I is paid to career linguists, at a baseline monthly rate of $100. Minimum qualifying proficiency for the baseline rate is set by each Service, but at not less than level 2 in listening and not less than level 2 in reading or speaking. Incremental increases of $25 are added for each level of proficiency attained above the minimum qualifier. A secondary program focus is to function as an incentive to any other members to maintain or increase their FL proficiency. FLPP-II is paid to other than career linguists (at a baseline monthly rate set by the Service concerned, but not above the FLPP-I Baseline Rate for careerist linguists). The minimum qualifying proficiency levels for FLPP-I apply equally to FLPP-II. Much of this information has been provided by the Uniformed Services Almanac. At the Service's option, incremental increases of $12.50 are added to the FLPP-II baseline rate for levels of proficiency attained above the minimum qualifier. Maximum monthly FLPP for proficiency in one foreign language is $200; for more than one foreign language it is $300.

91. Author is familiar with the Arlington County, VA, Public Education System, Glebe Elementary School. Arlington County schools are among the best funded and managed in the United States. While foreign language instruction in Arlington County elementary schools is available to students, it is an extra-curricular event provided once a week on a "pay and go" basis. Languages include Spanish, German, and French.

92. John A. Wickham, *Korea on the Brink*, Washington, DC: National Defense University Press, 1999, p. 175.

93. Feith.

94. Lawrence, as referenced by Wunderle, slide 15.

www.ingramcontent.com/pod-product-compliance
Lightning Source LLC
Chambersburg PA
CBHW081814280526
45789CB00008B/3125